MAD LIBS

CHRISTMAS FUN
MAD LIBS

by Roger Price & Leonard Stern

MAD LIBS
An Imprint of Penguin Random House LLC, New York

Mad Libs format and text copyright © 1985, 2001 by Penguin Random House LLC.
All rights reserved.

Concept created by Roger Price & Leonard Stern

Published by Mad Libs,
an imprint of Penguin Random House LLC, New York.
Manufactured in China.

Visit us online at www.penguinrandomhouse.com.

ISBN 9780515157093
7 9 10 8

INSTRUCTIONS

MAD LIBS® is a game for people who don't like games! It can be played by one, two, three, four, or forty.

• RIDICULOUSLY SIMPLE DIRECTIONS

In this tablet you will find stories containing blank spaces where words are left out. One player, the READER, selects one of these stories. The READER does not tell anyone what the story is about. Instead, he/she asks the other players, the WRITERS, to give him/her words. These words are used to fill in the blank spaces in the story.

• TO PLAY

The READER asks each WRITER in turn to call out a word—an adjective or a noun or whatever the space calls for—and uses them to fill in the blank spaces in the story. The result is a MAD LIBS® game.

When the READER then reads the completed MAD LIBS® game to the other players, they will discover that they have written a story that is fantastic, screamingly funny, shocking, silly, crazy, or just plain dumb—depending upon which words each WRITER called out.

• EXAMPLE (*Before* and *After*)

"_____!" he said _____
             EXCLAMATION   ADVERB

as he jumped into his convertible _____ and
                                              NOUN

drove off with his _____ wife.
                              ADJECTIVE

"_____**OUCH**_____!" he said _____**STUPIDLY**_____
             EXCLAMATION   ADVERB

as he jumped into his convertible _____**CAT**_____ and
                                              NOUN

drove off with his _____**BRAVE**_____ wife.
                              ADJECTIVE

In case you have forgotten what adjectives, adverbs, nouns, and verbs are, here is a quick review:

An ADJECTIVE describes something or somebody. *Lumpy, soft, ugly, messy,* and *short* are adjectives.

An ADVERB tells how something is done. It modifies a verb and usually ends in "ly." *Modestly, stupidly, greedily,* and *carefully* are adverbs.

A NOUN is the name of a person, place, or thing. *Sidewalk, umbrella, bridle, bathtub,* and *nose* are nouns.

A VERB is an action word. *Run, pitch, jump,* and *swim* are verbs. Put the verbs in past tense if the directions say PAST TENSE. *Ran, pitched, jumped,* and *swam* are verbs in the past tense.

When we ask for A PLACE, we mean any sort of place: a country or city (*Spain, Cleveland*) or a room (*bathroom, kitchen*).

An EXCLAMATION or SILLY WORD is any sort of funny sound, gasp, grunt, or outcry, like *Wow!, Ouch!, Whomp!, Ick!,* and *Gadzooks!*

When we ask for specific words, like a NUMBER, a COLOR, an ANIMAL, or a PART OF THE BODY, we mean a word that is one of those things, like *seven, blue, horse,* or *head.*

When we ask for a PLURAL, it means more than one. For example, *cat* pluralized is *cats.*

MAD LIBS® is fun to play with friends, but you can also play it by yourself! To begin with, DO NOT look at the story on the page below. Fill in the blanks on this page with the words called for. Then, using the words you have selected, fill in the blank spaces in the story.

Now you've created your own hilarious MAD LIBS® game!

SELECTING A TREE

ADJECTIVE _____

ADJECTIVE _____

NOUN _____

PLURAL NOUN _____

PLURAL NOUN _____

NOUN _____

NOUN _____

NOUN _____

ADJECTIVE _____

NOUN _____

NUMBER _____

PLURAL NOUN _____

NOUN _____

COLOR _____

COLOR _____

NOUN _____

PERSON IN ROOM _____

PERSON IN ROOM _____

MAD LIBS

SELECTING A TREE

No Christmas season can be really _____ unless you have
                                         ADJECTIVE

a/an _____ tree in your _____. If you live in a city,
         ADJECTIVE   NOUN

you will see many vacant _____ filled with hundreds of
                                  PLURAL NOUN

_____ for sale. If you live in the country, you can get
PLURAL NOUN

your own _____ right out of the forest. Go out with
                 NOUN

a/an _____ and _____, and when you see a/an
         NOUN   NOUN

_____ tree you like, you can dig it up and plant it in a/an
ADJECTIVE

_____. Then you can use it for _____ years. To make
NOUN   NUMBER

sure your tree is fresh, shake the branches and see if the _____
                                                                  PLURAL NOUN

fall off onto the _____. And make sure the tree is very
                         NOUN

_____. Nothing looks worse than a/an _____ tree.
COLOR   COLOR

Just follow these directions and you can have a perfectly beautiful

_____ in your front room for weeks. Remember, poems
NOUN

and Mad Libs are made by fools like _____, but only
                                          PERSON IN ROOM

_____ can make a tree.
PERSON IN ROOM

MAD LIBS® is fun to play with friends, but you can also play it by yourself! To begin with, DO NOT look at the story on the page below. Fill in the blanks on this page with the words called for. Then, using the words you have selected, fill in the blank spaces in the story.

Now you've created your own hilarious MAD LIBS® game!

DECORATING THE TREE

PERSON IN ROOM _____

VERB _____

PERSON IN ROOM _____

PLURAL NOUN _____

PERSON IN ROOM _____

TYPE OF FOOD (PLURAL) _____

TYPE OF FOOD (PLURAL) _____

PLURAL NOUN _____

ADJECTIVE _____

PLURAL NOUN _____

ADJECTIVE _____

NOUN _____

ADJECTIVE _____

ADJECTIVE _____

NOUN _____

PLURAL NOUN _____

NOUN _____

EXCLAMATION _____

MAD LIBS®
DECORATING THE TREE

Many people decorate their Christmas tree on Christmas Eve. Last

year _____ had a party and everyone helped _____
   PERSON IN ROOM   VERB

the tree. _____ brought tinsel and _____. And
       PERSON IN ROOM   PLURAL NOUN

_____ brought lots of fresh _____ and
PERSON IN ROOM   TYPE OF FOOD (PLURAL)

candy _____ to put on the tree. The most important
     TYPE OF FOOD (PLURAL)

decoration, of course, is the string of colored electric _____.
                                                     PLURAL NOUN

A few dozen lights make any tree look _____. And most stores
                                       ADJECTIVE

sell round, sparkly _____ and little _____ balls to
                 PLURAL NOUN   ADJECTIVE

hang on the branches. But the hardest decoration to pick is the one

that goes right on top. Once that _____ is up, you know that
                                      NOUN

the _____ season has officially started. Of course, if you are
     ADJECTIVE

too _____ to have a tree for Christmas, you can decorate your
     ADJECTIVE

_____ or hang _____ on your _____.
   NOUN   PLURAL NOUN   NOUN

Then the neighbors will say, " _____!"
                                 EXCLAMATION

MAD LIBS® is fun to play with friends, but you can also play it by yourself! To begin with, DO NOT look at the story on the page below. Fill in the blanks on this page with the words called for. Then, using the words you have selected, fill in the blank spaces in the story.

Now you've created your own hilarious MAD LIBS® game!

HOW TO WRAP A PRESENT

ADJECTIVE _____

PLURAL NOUN _____

ADJECTIVE _____

NOUN _____

PLURAL NOUN _____

VERB _____

NOUN _____

ADVERB _____

NOUN _____

COLOR _____

NOUN _____

ADJECTIVE _____

VERB _____

ADJECTIVE _____

PLURAL NOUN _____

ADJECTIVE _____

EXCLAMATION _____

ADJECTIVE _____

MAD LIBS®
HOW TO WRAP
A PRESENT

Before you start to wrap your Christmas present, make sure you have

plenty of _____ paper and lots of little _____ to
      ADJECTIVE   PLURAL NOUN

stick on the package. If you are wrapping something _____,
                 ADJECTIVE

such as a/an _____, it is best to tape _____ around
         NOUN   PLURAL NOUN

any parts that might _____. Then take brown wrapping
               VERB

_____ and wrap it very _____. Take care that
   NOUN   ADVERB

there is not a/an _____ poking out anywhere. Now take the
         NOUN

expensive _____ paper that you bought at the _____
      COLOR   NOUN

store and make a/an _____ package. Finally, put stickers on
         ADJECTIVE

that say "Do not _____ until Christmas" and put it under
         VERB

the tree with all the other _____ _____. Then
         ADJECTIVE   PLURAL NOUN

on Christmas morning, when you see all your _____ relatives
              ADJECTIVE

opening their packages and saying, "_____!" you will feel
          EXCLAMATION

positively _____.
    ADJECTIVE

MAD LIBS® is fun to play with friends, but you can also play it by yourself! To begin with, DO NOT look at the story on the page below. Fill in the blanks on this page with the words called for. Then, using the words you have selected, fill in the blank spaces in the story.

Now you've created your own hilarious MAD LIBS® game!

WHAT TO GET PEOPLE FOR CHRISTMAS

ADJECTIVE _____

PLURAL NOUN _____

NOUN _____

NOUN _____

ADJECTIVE _____

NOUN _____

VERB _____

NOUN _____

A PLACE _____

VERB _____

PLURAL NOUN _____

PERSON IN ROOM (FEMALE) _____

ARTICLE OF CLOTHING _____

CELEBRITY _____

PERSON IN ROOM (MALE) _____

PLURAL NOUN _____

PART OF THE BODY _____

NOUN _____

MAD LIBS®
WHAT TO GET PEOPLE FOR CHRISTMAS

One of the best things about Christmas is being able to pick out

_____ presents to give to your _____ and
   ADJECTIVE   PLURAL NOUN

relatives. But it's a problem because you don't want to give someone

a/an _____ when they really wanted a/an _____. Here
      NOUN   NOUN

are some _____ gift ideas. I bet your mother would like a new
          ADJECTIVE

electric _____ she could use to _____ her vegetables
        NOUN   VERB

or clean the _____ in (the) _____. If your father
          NOUN   A PLACE

likes to _____, he could use a new set of _____.
     VERB   PLURAL NOUN

If you want to get _____ a present, she needs a
          PERSON IN ROOM (FEMALE)

sports _____ designed by _____. And
    ARTICLE OF CLOTHING   CELEBRITY

_____ needs some _____ to keep his
PERSON IN ROOM (MALE)   PLURAL NOUN

_____ warm. But no matter what you give, remember it is the
PART OF THE BODY

_____ behind the gift that counts.
   NOUN

MAD LIBS® is fun to play with friends, but you can also play it by yourself! To begin with, DO NOT look at the story on the page below. Fill in the blanks on this page with the words called for. Then, using the words you have selected, fill in the blank spaces in the story.

Now you've created your own hilarious MAD LIBS® game!

CHRISTMAS DINNER

ADJECTIVE _____

NOUN _____

TYPE OF FOOD _____

PLURAL NOUN _____

TYPE OF LIQUID _____

ADJECTIVE _____

VERB _____

NOUN _____

PART OF THE BODY _____

NOUN _____

ADJECTIVE _____

NOUN _____

NUMBER _____

ADVERB _____

ADJECTIVE _____

PLURAL NOUN _____

EXCLAMATION _____

MAD LIBS®

CHRISTMAS DINNER

Everyone likes to have a/an _____ dinner on Christmas
ADJECTIVE

Day. Most people have a huge roast _____ stuffed with
NOUN

_____ dressing and served with mashed _____
TYPE OF FOOD   PLURAL NOUN

and plenty of hot brown _____. However, if you would
TYPE OF LIQUID

rather have a/an _____ turkey, here is how you should
ADJECTIVE

_____ it. First, make the dressing of old, dried _____
VERB   NOUN

crumbs. Then, put the dressing in the turkey's _____. Put it
PART OF THE BODY

in a big _____ and brush it with _____ butter. Next,
NOUN   ADJECTIVE

heat your _____ to _____ degrees. Put the turkey in
NOUN   NUMBER

and cook it very _____ for five hours. When you put it on
ADVERB

the table, the _____ aroma will make everyone smack their
ADJECTIVE

_____ and say, "_____!"
PLURAL NOUN   EXCLAMATION

From CHRISTMAS FUN MAD LIBS® • Copyright © 2001, 1985 by Penguin Random House LLC.

MAD LIBS® is fun to play with friends, but you can also play it by yourself! To begin with, DO NOT look at the story on the page below. Fill in the blanks on this page with the words called for. Then, using the words you have selected, fill in the blank spaces in the story.

Now you've created your own hilarious MAD LIBS® game!

TOYS FOR THE KIDS

ADJECTIVE _____

PLURAL NOUN _____

ADJECTIVE _____

SILLY WORD _____

PLURAL NOUN _____

NUMBER _____

VERB _____

LETTER OF THE ALPHABET _____

PLURAL NOUN _____

NOUN _____

ANIMAL _____

NOUN _____

NOUN _____

ADJECTIVE _____

ADJECTIVE _____

ADJECTIVE _____

PLURAL NOUN _____

MAD LIBS®

TOYS FOR THE KIDS

Today's parents buy very _____ toys for their little
                                    ADJECTIVE

_____ . Fifty years ago, children got _____
      PLURAL NOUN   ADJECTIVE

electric trains or baby dolls that said, "_____ ," when you
                                                SILLY WORD

squeezed them. Now children only want electronic _____ .
                                                        PLURAL NOUN

Even _____ -year-olds know how to _____ a computer.
          NUMBER   VERB

Or a/an _____ -Phone. Kids want remote-controlled
          LETTER OF THE ALPHABET

_____ . Or tiny robot monsters that can blow up your
   PLURAL NOUN

_____ or take your _____ prisoner. Everything
      NOUN   ANIMAL

has to have a silicon _____ in it and be operated by a nine-
                              NOUN

volt _____ . By the year 2030, all American children will
          NOUN

probably want to have their own _____ space shuttle and
                                        ADJECTIVE

_____ robot playmate manufactured by General Motors.
   ADJECTIVE

In fact, by that time maybe children will be manufactured by

a/an _____ assembly line and will be operated by nine-volt
          ADJECTIVE

_____ .
   PLURAL NOUN

MAD LIBS® is fun to play with friends, but you can also play it by yourself! To begin with, DO NOT look at the story on the page below. Fill in the blanks on this page with the words called for. Then, using the words you have selected, fill in the blank spaces in the story.

Now you've created your own hilarious MAD LIBS® game!

A LETTER TO SANTA

PERSON IN ROOM _____

NOUN _____

ADJECTIVE _____

VERB _____

EXCLAMATION _____

VERB (PAST TENSE) _____

VERB (PAST TENSE) _____

PLURAL NOUN _____

ADJECTIVE _____

NOUN _____

ADJECTIVE _____

NOUN _____

PERSON IN ROOM _____

ADJECTIVE _____

ADJECTIVE _____

ARTICLE OF CLOTHING _____

MAD LIBS®

A LETTER TO SANTA

Dear Santa,

My name is _____, and all year I have been a very, very
  PERSON IN ROOM

good _____. I have been _____ at school, and
  NOUN   ADJECTIVE

when my teacher asked me to _____ the whiteboard, I
  VERB

just said, "_____!" I have not _____
  EXCLAMATION   VERB (PAST TENSE)

or _____. Not even once. And I have helped a lot
  VERB (PAST TENSE)

of old _____ cross the street. Because I have been so
  PLURAL NOUN

_____, I am sure you are going to bring me a brand-new
  ADJECTIVE

_____ with _____ wheels. I would also like to have
  NOUN   ADJECTIVE

a/an _____ racket. And a secret microphone so I can spy
  NOUN

on _____ and learn all his/her _____ secrets. Well,
  PERSON IN ROOM   ADJECTIVE

Santa, I know you will put all these _____ presents in my
  ADJECTIVE

_____ on Christmas. Or else I will have been good
  ARTICLE OF CLOTHING

for nothing.

MAD LIBS® is fun to play with friends, but you can also play it by yourself! To begin with, DO NOT look at the story on the page below. Fill in the blanks on this page with the words called for. Then, using the words you have selected, fill in the blank spaces in the story.

Now you've created your own hilarious MAD LIBS® game!

A VISIT WITH SANTA AT THE NORTH POLE

ADJECTIVE _____

PLURAL NOUN _____

FIRST NAME (FEMALE) _____

ADJECTIVE _____

NUMBER _____

PLURAL NOUN _____

PLURAL NOUN _____

VEHICLE _____

ADJECTIVE _____

ANIMAL (PLURAL) _____

NOUN _____

NOUN _____

ARTICLE OF CLOTHING (PLURAL) _____

NUMBER _____

VERB _____

MAD LIBS®
A VISIT WITH SANTA
AT THE NORTH POLE

Santa Claus has a very _____ life. He lives at the North
ADJECTIVE

Pole surrounded by snow and _____. He is married
PLURAL NOUN

to _____ Claus and instead of children, they have
FIRST NAME (FEMALE)

_____ little elves. This way, Santa can get help in his workshop
ADJECTIVE

for only _____ dollars an hour. The elves work eleven months
NUMBER

a year making _____ and _____ for Santa
PLURAL NOUN   PLURAL NOUN

to give children on Christmas. On Christmas Eve, the elves load up

Santa's _____ with the _____ presents. Then Santa
VEHICLE   ADJECTIVE

hitches it to his team of _____ and goes sailing through
ANIMAL (PLURAL)

the sky. When he sees a child's house, he lands on the _____
NOUN

and slides down the chimney, landing on the _____. Then
NOUN

he puts the presents into the _____ that the
ARTICLE OF CLOTHING (PLURAL)

children have hung on the mantelpiece. After he does this _____
NUMBER

times, he goes home to get ready to _____.
VERB

MAD LIBS® is fun to play with friends, but you can also play it by yourself! To begin with, DO NOT look at the story on the page below. Fill in the blanks on this page with the words called for. Then, using the words you have selected, fill in the blank spaces in the story.

Now you've created your own hilarious MAD LIBS® game!

GOING TO SEE SANTA

PERSON IN ROOM _____

NUMBER _____

PART OF THE BODY _____

NOUN _____

NOUN _____

ADJECTIVE _____

NOUN _____

ADJECTIVE _____

COLOR _____

ARTICLE OF CLOTHING (PLURAL) _____

NOUN _____

SILLY WORD _____

NOUN _____

EXCLAMATION _____

ANIMAL _____

NOUN _____

PLURAL NOUN _____

ADVERB _____

MAD LIBS®

GOING TO SEE SANTA

Yesterday I took my friend _____ to see Santa Claus at the
PERSON IN ROOM

department store. He/She is only _____ years old, so I had to
NUMBER

be sure to hold on to his/her _____ whenever we crossed
PART OF THE BODY

a/an _____. When we got to the _____, there was
NOUN NOUN

a long line of _____ kids waiting to talk to Santa, who was
ADJECTIVE

sitting on a platform in the _____ department. Santa Claus
NOUN

is a big, fat, _____ man with a/an _____ beard who
ADJECTIVE COLOR

dresses in bright red _____. Whenever a little
ARTICLE OF CLOTHING (PLURAL)

kid came up, Santa would sit the child on his _____ and say,
NOUN

"_____." Then he would say, "Now, have you been a good
SILLY WORD

little _____?" And the kid would say, "_____!"
NOUN EXCLAMATION

Then Santa would say, "And what do you want for Christmas?" And

the kid would say, "I want a/an _____," or "I want an electric
ANIMAL

_____," or "I want some little toy _____." Then
NOUN PLURAL NOUN

Santa would say, "You bet," and the kid would run _____
ADVERB

back to his or her parents.

From CHRISTMAS FUN MAD LIBS® • Copyright © 2001, 1985 by Penguin Random House LLC.

MAD LIBS® is fun to play with friends, but you can also play it by yourself! To begin with, DO NOT look at the story on the page below. Fill in the blanks on this page with the words called for. Then, using the words you have selected, fill in the blank spaces in the story.

Now you've created your own hilarious MAD LIBS® game!

THE TWELVE DAYS OF CHRISTMAS

NOUN _____

NOUN _____

ADJECTIVE _____

NOUN _____

ANIMAL (PLURAL) _____

NOUN _____

NUMBER _____

ADJECTIVE _____

PLURAL NOUN _____

PLURAL NOUN _____

NOUN _____

PLURAL NOUN _____

ADJECTIVE _____

NOUN _____

MAD LIBS®
THE TWELVE DAYS
OF CHRISTMAS

On the first day of Christmas, my true love gave to me a/an

_____ in a/an _____ tree. On the second day of
    NOUN   NOUN

Christmas, my true love gave to me two _____ doves and
                                               ADJECTIVE

a/an _____ in a pear tree. On the third day of Christmas,
           NOUN

my true love gave to me three French _____, two turtle
                                      ANIMAL (PLURAL)

doves, and a/an _____ in a pear tree. On the fourth day of
                NOUN

Christmas, my true love gave to me _____ _____
                                          NUMBER   ADJECTIVE

_____, three French _____, two turtle
  PLURAL NOUN   PLURAL NOUN

doves, and a/an _____ in a pear tree. On the fifth day of
                NOUN

Christmas, my true love gave to me five golden _____,
                                          PLURAL NOUN

four calling birds, three _____ hens, two turtle doves, and
                              ADJECTIVE

a/an _____ in a pear tree.
           NOUN

MAD LIBS® is fun to play with friends, but you can also play it by yourself! To begin with, DO NOT look at the story on the page below. Fill in the blanks on this page with the words called for. Then, using the words you have selected, fill in the blank spaces in the story.

Now you've created your own hilarious MAD LIBS® game!

CHRISTMAS CAROLS

ADJECTIVE _____

ADJECTIVE _____

ADVERB _____

PLURAL NOUN _____

SILLY WORD (PLURAL) _____

PLURAL NOUN _____

NOUN _____

COLOR _____

A PLACE _____

PLURAL NOUN _____

OCCUPATION (PLURAL) _____

ADJECTIVE _____

PLURAL NOUN _____

CITY _____

A PLACE _____

NUMBER _____

PERSON IN ROOM _____

MAD LIBS®

CHRISTMAS CAROLS

This Christmas, our _____ glee club is planning a/an
                         ADJECTIVE

_____ program of Christmas carols. We all sing very
    ADJECTIVE

_____ and are going to sing on the streets and collect
    ADVERB

_____ to feed the poor, hungry _____ in
  PLURAL NOUN   SILLY WORD (PLURAL)

Transylvania. Our program will start with "Jingle _____,"
                                                    PLURAL NOUN

followed by "Rudolph, the Red-Nosed _____," "I'm Dreaming
                                         NOUN

of a/an _____ Christmas," and "Santa Claus Is Coming to
            COLOR

(the) _____." My favorites, however, are "Deck the Halls with
       A PLACE

Boughs of _____," "We Three _____ of
             PLURAL NOUN   OCCUPATION (PLURAL)

Orient Are," and "Walking in a/an _____ Wonderland." If it
                                     ADJECTIVE

goes well, we can form a group, call ourselves the _____,
                                                      PLURAL NOUN

and do concerts in _____ or even in (the) _____.
                       CITY   A PLACE

We'll have _____ fans and make a video. We'll be as famous as
              NUMBER

_____.
PERSON IN ROOM

MAD LIBS® is fun to play with friends, but you can also play it by yourself! To begin with, DO NOT look at the story on the page below. Fill in the blanks on this page with the words called for. Then, using the words you have selected, fill in the blank spaces in the story.

Now you've created your own hilarious MAD LIBS® game!

A TRANSYLVANIAN NEW YEAR'S

ADJECTIVE _____

NOUN _____

NOUN _____

PLURAL NOUN _____

PLURAL NOUN _____

ADVERB _____

PLURAL NOUN _____

ADJECTIVE _____

ANIMAL _____

TYPE OF FOOD _____

NUMBER _____

VERB _____

SILLY WORD _____

NUMBER _____

PLURAL NOUN _____

NOUN _____

ADJECTIVE _____

MAD LIBS®
A TRANSYLVANIAN NEW YEAR'S

New Year's Day in Transylvania is the most _____ holiday
ADJECTIVE

of the year. All the _____ shops and _____
NOUN   NOUN

factories are shut down, and the _____ dance in the
PLURAL NOUN

streets. The locals, who are called _____, spend all day
PLURAL NOUN

dancing _____. And some Transylvanians, who are called
ADVERB

_____, prepare a/an _____ feast. New Year's
PLURAL NOUN   ADJECTIVE

dinner always features a wild roast _____. It is skinned,
ANIMAL

put in an oven, and covered with _____. Then it is cooked
TYPE OF FOOD

for _____ hours. After dinner, a contest is held to see which
NUMBER

Transylvanian can _____ the loudest. The winner is given the
VERB

title of "_____." Then famous Count Dracula himself raffles
SILLY WORD

off _____ _____ to help pay the _____ who
NUMBER   PLURAL NOUN   NOUN

has to come in the next day and clean up the whole _____
ADJECTIVE

country.

MAD LIBS® is fun to play with friends, but you can also play it by yourself! To begin with, DO NOT look at the story on the page below. Fill in the blanks on this page with the words called for. Then, using the words you have selected, fill in the blank spaces in the story.

Now you've created your own hilarious MAD LIBS® game!

NEW YEAR'S RESOLUTION

NOUN _____

NOUN _____

VERB _____

TYPE OF FOOD _____

PLURAL NOUN _____

PLURAL NOUN _____

ADJECTIVE _____

PLURAL NOUN _____

VERB _____

TYPE OF LIQUID _____

PART OF THE BODY _____

ARTICLE OF CLOTHING _____

ADJECTIVE _____

ADVERB _____

ADJECTIVE _____

MAD LIBS®
NEW YEAR'S RESOLUTION

I resolve that in the next year I will eat all my ＿＿＿＿＿＿＿＿, just
                                                        NOUN
like my mother says. I promise to help bathe my pet ＿＿＿＿＿＿＿＿
                                                            NOUN
and help ＿＿＿＿＿＿＿＿ the dishes after dinner. I will not eat any
              VERB
＿＿＿＿＿＿＿＿ that contains cholesterol or ＿＿＿＿＿＿＿＿. I will
TYPE OF FOOD   PLURAL NOUN
be polite and thoughtful and will clear the ＿＿＿＿＿＿＿＿ after
                                                PLURAL NOUN
meals. I will do a/an ＿＿＿＿＿＿＿＿ deed every day. I will also be
                          ADJECTIVE
polite to any ＿＿＿＿＿＿＿＿ who are older than I am. And I will
                  PLURAL NOUN
never, never ＿＿＿＿＿＿＿＿ my dog's tail or pour ＿＿＿＿＿＿＿＿
                  VERB   TYPE OF LIQUID
on my cat. I will also try to brush my ＿＿＿＿＿＿＿＿ and shine
                                            PART OF THE BODY
my ＿＿＿＿＿＿＿＿＿＿＿＿ every day. I promise to be really
      ARTICLE OF CLOTHING
＿＿＿＿＿＿＿＿ so I can live ＿＿＿＿＿＿＿＿ for the next twelve
  ADJECTIVE   ADVERB
months. Then I'll be a truly happy, ＿＿＿＿＿＿＿＿ person.
                                        ADJECTIVE

MAD LIBS® is fun to play with friends, but you can also play it by yourself! To begin with, DO NOT look at the story on the page below. Fill in the blanks on this page with the words called for. Then, using the words you have selected, fill in the blank spaces in the story.

Now you've created your own hilarious MAD LIBS® game!

SCROOGE

PERSON IN ROOM _____

FOREIGN COUNTRY _____

NOUN _____

PLURAL NOUN _____

NUMBER _____

SILLY WORD _____

ADJECTIVE _____

NUMBER _____

ADJECTIVE _____

NOUN _____

NOUN _____

NUMBER _____

ADJECTIVE _____

ADJECTIVE _____

NOUN _____

FIRST NAME (MALE) _____

COLOR _____

EXCLAMATION _____

MAD●LIBS®

SCROOGE

You have just read *A Christmas Carol* by _____. Years ago

PERSON IN ROOM

in London, _____, lived a mean, stingy _____

FOREIGN COUNTRY ___ NOUN

named Scrooge. He was so stingy, he saved _____. In fact,

PLURAL NOUN

he had more than _____ of them. When anyone mentioned

NUMBER

Christmas, Scrooge said, "Bah! _____." He had a/an

SILLY WORD

_____ bookkeeper named Bob Cratchit, and Scrooge made

ADJECTIVE

him work _____ hours a day. One Christmas Eve, Mr. Scrooge

NUMBER

had a dream. He saw the Ghost of Christmas Past, who showed him

what a/an _____ _____ he had been. Then the

ADJECTIVE ___ NOUN

_____ of Christmas Present showed Scrooge the miserable

NOUN

home of Bob Cratchit and poor Tiny Tim. Tiny Tim had a temperature

of _____ degrees. Then Scrooge met the Ghost of Christmas

NUMBER

_____, who took him to a/an _____ cemetery,

ADJECTIVE ___ ADJECTIVE

where Scrooge saw his own _____. He also saw the grave of

NOUN

Tiny _____. Scrooge turned _____ and shouted,

FIRST NAME (MALE) ___ COLOR

"_____!"

EXCLAMATION

MAD LIBS® is fun to play with friends, but you can also play it by yourself! To begin with, DO NOT look at the story on the page below. Fill in the blanks on this page with the words called for. Then, using the words you have selected, fill in the blank spaces in the story.

Now you've created your own hilarious MAD LIBS® game!

SCROOGE
(CONTINUED)

NOUN _____

NOUN _____

NOUN _____

NOUN _____

ARTICLE OF CLOTHING _____

ANIMAL _____

ADJECTIVE _____

NOUN _____

NOUN _____

NOUN _____

ADJECTIVE _____

PLURAL NOUN _____

ADJECTIVE _____

PLURAL NOUN _____

ADJECTIVE _____

NOUN _____

NOUN _____

CELEBRITY _____

MAD LIBS®
SCROOGE
(CONTINUED)

The next morning when the _____ came up, Scrooge jumped
NOUN

out of his _____ and said, "I am a changed _____.
NOUN   NOUN

I only hope it is not too late for me to become a kindly, generous

_____." He put on his _____, rushed
NOUN   ARTICLE OF CLOTHING

to the butcher shop, and said, "Give me the biggest _____
ANIMAL

you have." Then he bought cakes and _____ cookies and
ADJECTIVE

a beautiful _____ pudding. He put everything in a big
NOUN

_____, rushed to Bob Cratchit's house, and pounded on
NOUN

the _____. When Bob Cratchit opened the door, Scrooge
NOUN

said, "_____ Christmas, Bob. I have _____ for
ADJECTIVE   PLURAL NOUN

everyone, including Tiny Tim." And they all had a/an _____
ADJECTIVE

dinner and sang jolly _____. Scrooge had indeed changed
PLURAL NOUN

from a/an _____ skinflint into a wonderful _____.
ADJECTIVE   NOUN

He gave Tiny Tim a solid gold _____, and Tiny Tim said,
NOUN

"Merry Christmas, and may _____ bless us every one . . ."
CELEBRITY

MAD LIBS® is fun to play with friends, but you can also play it by yourself! To begin with, DO NOT look at the story on the page below. Fill in the blanks on this page with the words called for. Then, using the words you have selected, fill in the blank spaces in the story.

Now you've created your own hilarious MAD LIBS® game!

THE SCHOOL PARTY

ADJECTIVE _____

NOUN _____

PERSON IN ROOM _____

NOUN _____

NOUN _____

PERSON IN ROOM _____

CELEBRITY _____

NOUN _____

PLURAL NOUN _____

PERSON IN ROOM _____

ADJECTIVE _____

TYPE OF FOOD _____

TYPE OF LIQUID _____

ADJECTIVE _____

NUMBER _____

PLURAL NOUN _____

PERSON IN ROOM _____

EXCLAMATION _____

MAD LIBS®

THE SCHOOL PARTY

We had a/an _____ Christmas party at school last year. Our
       ADJECTIVE

_____ teacher, _____, let us use the _____
  NOUN   PERSON IN ROOM   NOUN

room. And my favorite _____ teacher, _____, was
            NOUN   PERSON IN ROOM

in charge of the decorations. We all drew pictures of _____
                                   CELEBRITY

on colored paper and hung them on a long _____. Then we
                                 NOUN

cut out stars, snowflakes, and _____ and pasted them on
                       PLURAL NOUN

the windows. Then _____, who is my math teacher, made
            PERSON IN ROOM

the _____ refreshments. We had burgers and _____
    ADJECTIVE   TYPE OF FOOD

and cups of hot _____. Our principal bought a really
         TYPE OF LIQUID

_____ tree that was _____ feet tall. And everyone put
  ADJECTIVE   NUMBER

their _____ under it. _____ dressed up like Santa
    PLURAL NOUN   PERSON IN ROOM

Claus and said, "_____!"
         EXCLAMATION

MAD LIBS® is fun to play with friends, but you can also play it by yourself! To begin with, DO NOT look at the story on the page below. Fill in the blanks on this page with the words called for. Then, using the words you have selected, fill in the blank spaces in the story.

Now you've created your own hilarious MAD LIBS® game!

THANK-YOU LETTERS

FIRST NAME (FEMALE) _____

ADJECTIVE _____

NOUN _____

PLURAL NOUN _____

PART OF THE BODY _____

ADJECTIVE _____

ADJECTIVE _____

FIRST NAME (MALE) _____

NOUN _____

PLURAL NOUN _____

ADJECTIVE _____

PLURAL NOUN _____

ADJECTIVE _____

PLURAL NOUN _____

NOUN _____

CELEBRITY _____

MAD LIBS®

THANK-YOU LETTERS

Dear Auntie _____,
          FIRST NAME (FEMALE)

I want to thank you for sending me the _____ gift. I never had
                                          ADJECTIVE

a/an _____ before. I can use it to fix all my _____.
       NOUN   PLURAL NOUN

It will also keep my _____ warm if we have any _____
                      PART OF THE BODY   ADJECTIVE

weather.

        Your _____ nephew,
              ADJECTIVE

        _____
        FIRST NAME (MALE)

Dear Grandpa and Grandma,

I really like the _____ you sent me. It must have cost a lot of
                    NOUN

_____. All the kids around here have _____
PLURAL NOUN   ADJECTIVE

computers. But mine is the only one that has six different

_____. It will help me do my _____ homework,
PLURAL NOUN   ADJECTIVE

and I know I will get higher _____ this year. Mom says I
                               PLURAL NOUN

can come to your _____ for a visit next summer.
                    NOUN

        Signed, _____
                 CELEBRITY

From CHRISTMAS FUN MAD LIBS® • Copyright © 2001, 1985 by Penguin Random House LLC.

MAD LIBS® is fun to play with friends, but you can also play it by yourself! To begin with, DO NOT look at the story on the page below. Fill in the blanks on this page with the words called for. Then, using the words you have selected, fill in the blank spaces in the story.

Now you've created your own hilarious MAD LIBS® game!

HOLIDAY TRAVELING

PLURAL NOUN _____

PLURAL NOUN _____

ADJECTIVE _____

PLURAL NOUN _____

NOUN _____

ADJECTIVE _____

A PLACE _____

A PLACE _____

NUMBER _____

PLURAL NOUN _____

NUMBER _____

PLURAL NOUN _____

PART OF THE BODY _____

ADJECTIVE _____

PLURAL NOUN _____

PLURAL NOUN _____

MAD LIBS

HOLIDAY TRAVELING

During the holidays, more _____ go back home to visit
their _____ than at any other time. Between Christmas and
_____ Year's Day, the airlines pack the _____ in
like sardines in a/an _____. There are a lot of _____
"no frill" airlines that will take you from (the) _____ to (the)
_____ for only _____ dollars. These airlines do not
give you any _____. And you can only take _____
pieces of luggage. They also have smaller _____, and
you often have to sit on someone else's _____. It is very
_____ to travel during the holidays, but it is worth it to
make your _____ happy. Don't forget to make your
_____ early.

From CHRISTMAS FUN MAD LIBS® • Copyright © 2001, 1985 by Penguin Random House LLC.

MAD LIBS® is fun to play with friends, but you can also play it by yourself! To begin with, DO NOT look at the story on the page below. Fill in the blanks on this page with the words called for. Then, using the words you have selected, fill in the blank spaces in the story.

Now you've created your own hilarious MAD LIBS® game!

NEW YEAR'S BOWL GAMES

CITY _____

ANIMAL (PLURAL) _____

A PLACE _____

ANIMAL (PLURAL) _____

NOUN _____

CITY _____

ANIMAL (PLURAL) _____

CITY _____

PLURAL NOUN _____

ANIMAL _____

TYPE OF FOOD _____

CITY _____

CITY _____

ANIMAL (PLURAL) _____

NOUN _____

PERSON IN ROOM _____

NOUN _____

COLOR _____

On New Year's Day, there are always a lot of football games. On television, they interrupt the game with commercials every few minutes. This year the _____ _____ are
\(\quad\quad\quad\quad\quad\quad\quad\quad\quad\) CITY \(\quad\quad\quad\) ANIMAL (PLURAL)
playing the _____ _____ in the famous
\(\quad\quad\quad\quad\quad\) A PLACE \(\quad\quad\) ANIMAL (PLURAL)
_____ Bowl. And the _____ _____ are
NOUN \(\quad\quad\quad\quad\quad\quad\quad\) CITY \(\quad\quad\) ANIMAL (PLURAL)
matched up against the nation's number one team, the_____
\(\quad\quad\quad\quad\quad\quad\quad\quad\quad\quad\quad\quad\quad\quad\quad\quad\quad\quad\) CITY
_____. They will be playing in the _____ Bowl.
PLURAL NOUN \(\quad\quad\quad\quad\quad\quad\quad\quad\quad\) ANIMAL
But the game that everyone is talking about is the _____
\(\quad\quad\quad\quad\quad\quad\quad\quad\quad\quad\quad\quad\quad\quad\quad\quad\) TYPE OF FOOD
Bowl. There, the _____ Cowboys will play the hard-
\(\quad\quad\quad\quad\quad\) CITY
hitting _____ _____, whose quarterback is
\(\quad\quad\) CITY \(\quad\quad\) ANIMAL (PLURAL)
the super-_____ _____. They will play in the
\(\quad\quad\quad\) NOUN \(\quad\quad\) PERSON IN ROOM
fabulous Houston Astro-_____, which has a sliding roof
\(\quad\quad\quad\quad\quad\quad\quad\quad\) NOUN
and _____ AstroTurf.
\(\quad\) COLOR

MAD LIBS® is fun to play with friends, but you can also play it by yourself! To begin with, DO NOT look at the story on the page below. Fill in the blanks on this page with the words called for. Then, using the words you have selected, fill in the blank spaces in the story.

Now you've created your own hilarious MAD LIBS® game!

CHRISTMAS VACATION

ADJECTIVE _____

ADJECTIVE _____

ADJECTIVE _____

NOUN _____

NOUN _____

NOUN _____

NOUN _____

ADJECTIVE _____

VERB _____

NOUN _____

PLURAL NOUN _____

NOUN _____

PLURAL NOUN _____

NOUN _____

PLURAL NOUN _____

NOUN _____

A PLACE _____

COLOR _____

MAD LIBS®

CHRISTMAS VACATION

This year my entire family—my sister, my _____ brother, and
ADJECTIVE

my parents—are planning to spend the holidays in the _____
ADJECTIVE

mountains in a/an _____ cabin built by my _____.
ADJECTIVE _NOUN_

The cabin is in the middle of a huge _____ on the edge
NOUN

of a/an _____, which is always frozen at this time of the
NOUN

_____. If the ice is _____ enough, we will be able
NOUN _ADJECTIVE_

to _____ on it. We will decorate the big pine _____
VERB _NOUN_

in front of the cabin with Christmas _____. At night, we
PLURAL NOUN

will build a fire in the _____ and toast _____.
NOUN _PLURAL NOUN_

It promises to be a great _____. Next year I hope we can
NOUN

save up enough _____ so that we can afford to get on
PLURAL NOUN

a/an _____ and fly to (the) _____ and have a really
NOUN _A PLACE_

_____ Christmas.
COLOR

MAD LIBS® is fun to play with friends, but you can also play it by yourself! To begin with, DO NOT look at the story on the page below. Fill in the blanks on this page with the words called for. Then, using the words you have selected, fill in the blank spaces in the story.

Now you've created your own hilarious MAD LIBS® game!

THE NIGHT BEFORE CHRISTMAS

NOUN _____

ANIMAL _____

ANIMAL _____

PLURAL NOUN _____

TYPE OF FOOD (PLURAL) _____

PART OF THE BODY (PLURAL) _____

NOUN _____

NOUN _____

PERSON IN ROOM _____

VEHICLE _____

NUMBER _____

ANIMAL (PLURAL) _____

PLURAL NOUN _____

PART OF THE BODY _____

PART OF THE BODY _____

VERB (PAST TENSE) _____

VERB (PAST TENSE) _____

ADJECTIVE _____

MAD LIBS®
THE NIGHT BEFORE CHRISTMAS

'Twas the night before Christmas and all through the _____,

NOUN

not a/an _____ was stirring, not even a/an _____. The

ANIMAL   ANIMAL

children were nestled all snug in their _____, while visions

PLURAL NOUN

of _____ danced in their _____.

TYPE OF FOOD (PLURAL)   PART OF THE BODY (PLURAL)

When out on the lawn there arose such a clatter, I sprang from

my _____ to see what was the matter. I knew in a/an

NOUN

_____ it must be Saint _____, with his miniature

NOUN   PERSON IN ROOM

_____ and _____ tiny _____. He

VEHICLE   NUMBER   ANIMAL (PLURAL)

filled all our _____, then laying his _____ aside of

PLURAL NOUN   PART OF THE BODY

his _____, up the chimney he _____. But I

PART OF THE BODY   VERB (PAST TENSE)

heard him exclaim, as he _____ out of sight, "Merry

VERB (PAST TENSE)

Christmas to all and to all a/an _____ night."

ADJECTIVE